Discovering Cambridge: The Ultimate Guide for Beginners

Axel .M Garner

All rights reserved.

Copyright © 2024 Axel .M Garner

Discovering Cambridge: The Ultimate Guide for Beginners : Uncover the Charm and History of Cambridge with this Essential Starter Guide

Funny helpful tips:

Stay updated with the evolution of digital wallets; they're centralizing financial transactions and enhancing security.

When faced with adversity, remember that the strongest trees grow in the windiest conditions.

Introduction

Nestled along the serene banks of the River Cam, the picturesque city of Cambridge beckons with its rich history, iconic architecture, and a culture that seamlessly blends tradition with modernity. As you prepare to explore this charming city, let this travel guide serve as your companion, unveiling the treasures hidden within its cobbled streets and the timeless beauty of its world-renowned university.

Cambridge is a haven for cyclists, with its flat terrain and a network of cycling paths that wind through the heart of the city. Embrace the local lifestyle by renting a bike, allowing you to effortlessly navigate the enchanting streets and discover hidden gems at your own pace.

Prepare for the ever-changing British weather by packing layers. Whether the sun graces the city with its warmth or the clouds cast a gentle shadow, a light jacket and comfortable shoes will ensure you are ready to explore the city's wonders in any weather.

Immerse yourself in the local charm by staying in an Airbnb, offering a unique perspective on Cambridge life. Alternatively, indulge in the comfort of well-established hotels, where luxury meets convenience, providing a perfect retreat after a day of exploration.

Embark on a journey through time as you explore the city's storied past. Visit Cambridge University, a cornerstone of academia since its inception. Discover the architectural marvels of King's College, Trinity College, and St John's College, each contributing to the city's academic and cultural legacy.

Delve into the city's cultural tapestry with a visit to The Fitzwilliam Museum, showcasing art and antiquities from various eras. Stroll through The Market, where local vendors offer an array of delights. Conclude your day at The Eagle, a historic pub with an aviation-themed interior, immortalized for its role in scientific discovery.

Savor the culinary delights of Cambridge, from casual lunches to Michelin-starred feasts. Indulge in the local specialty, Chelsea buns, and discover the charm of afternoon tea in quaint tea rooms scattered across the city.

Navigate the serene River Cam, passing under iconic bridges like Magdalene Bridge, the Bridge of Sighs, and the Mathematical Bridge. Admire the architectural prowess of Trinity Bridge, King's College Bridge, and the Wren Bridge at St John's.

For the adventurous, consider a jump from one of the historic bridges. Marvel at the enigmatic Corpus Clock and explore Cambridge's diverse churches, including the Round Church, the Church of St Benet, and the grandeur of Great St Mary's.

Embrace the river culture with a punt along the Backs, where houseboats and boathouses line the water's edge. Admire the elegant swans that gracefully navigate the river, adding a touch of enchantment to your aquatic adventure.

Embark on a self-guided walking tour, discovering the city's hidden gems and secrets. Engage in family-friendly activities, fostering a love for exploration and learning in the younger travelers.

Uncover the vibrant arts scene with visits to local theaters, participation in festivals, and a rhythmic exploration of the city's music venues. Delight in the hidden gems and secrets that make Cambridge a city of endless discovery.

As you traverse the cobblestone streets and embrace the timeless allure of Cambridge, let this guide be your passport to an unforgettable journey, where each step reveals the essence of a city steeped in history and adorned with modern wonders. Welcome to Cambridge, a city that invites you to wander, wonder, and uncover its myriad charms.

Contents

Cyclists 1
BIKE HIRE 2
THE GREAT BRITISH WEATHER 4
WHAT TO PACK 5
COMFORTABLE SHOES 6
WHERE TO STAY 7
AIRBNB 8
HOTELS 9
LOCAL TRAVEL 11
E-bikes and scooters 12
KING'S COLLEGE 17
The view from Great St Mary's Tower 27

Cyclists

Cambridge is the city of bikes. That is probably the first thing to know. It is important to learn how to navigate the shared pavements and pathways. Cyclists should give way to pedestrians, nevertheless, be prepared to jump out of the way should one veer towards you. Cycle lanes are usually indicated by a bicycle painted on the pathway or a signpost close to the road. Do stay out of their way as much as possible as cyclists can speed along very fast.

BIKE HIRE

Cambridge has more than 85 miles of cycle lanes and 1 in 4 people cycle to work. Cycling is the main form of transport for most of the people who live and study here. A cyclist counting machine was installed in 2014 to mark Cambridge's contribution to the Tour de France visit. It is situated on Gonville Place by the side of the Parkers Piece and in December of 2016, the number of cyclists passing by exceeded one million.

Cycle rental

Rutland Cycling has great reviews. It is possible to hire a bike from the Cambridge Main station. Use a search engine to find other companies online and contact them in advance. Bike hire is busy, can be hectic and you may need to book in advance. It is recommended you wear a bike helmet as they can save your life if you fall off or get into an accident. In addition, the company Cambridge Bike Tours provides an entertaining way to see the sights.

THE GREAT BRITISH WEATHER

The British are famous globally for the never-ending discussion of the weather. The reason behind this is that it is so changeable! England, one of the four nations of the United Kingdom, is next to The Atlantic Ocean and mainland Europe, with six air masses converging at various times throughout the year from such diverse places as the Arctic and Africa. Our weather varies with the 'wind' as the year passes through the seasons. Be prepared for anything and bring an umbrella or be ready to buy one (from almost every store in the city) if a downpour greets you.

WHAT TO PACK

COMFORTABLE SHOES

Cambridge is flat, with an average elevation of only 47 feet (14 metres) above sea level; you can walk almost everywhere. Castle Mound is an excellent place to take a picnic to watch the May Ball, November fireworks or the sunrise or sunset. Find this by walking out of the city on Bridge Street, over Magdalene Bridge and up the hill. Turn right into the car park and you will see the grassy hill that is Castle Mound.

Layers

Bring layers so you can easily switch from cool to warm with the weather and always do a local weather check each day to confirm. Smart-casual comfortable clothes will take you anywhere and are what most locals wear.

WHERE TO STAY

AIRBNB

Airbnb is a great addition to the many hotels in Cambridge. Pricing varies between £35 - £500 or more per night for some places. When choosing where to stay, consider not only your budget but the distance and transport or walking route to the city centre. For example, a 30-minute walk along the River Cam is truly delightful, but a walk in and out of busy streets may not be so interesting. Get the postcode and search on maps to confirm where it is located. There is a fabulous recommended one-bed apartment, Riverside View (pictured above) overlooking the River Cam with a 30-minute walk along the river to the city centre.

HOTELS

There are many great hotels in the town.

The Fellows House and Madingley Hall are two such hotels. One for the architecture and the latter for the soft luxurious bed sheets.

The Gonville Hotel can be expensive; however, it is in the town centre and it is easy to walk everywhere.

The Varsity Hotel has a spa and gym and is right in the city. In summer it is a favourite place to watch the sun go down while sipping a cocktail at the rooftop bar.

The Premier Inn is a short walk into town along a busy road but can be a good value for money.

LOCAL TRAVEL

Buses

Buses in the UK are usually reliable, safe, and easy to use. Some bus stops have computerised tracking so you know almost exactly how long it will be until the next bus comes along. As always, planning your route, finding the bus stop, and getting the ticket before travel can help you have an enjoyable time and reduce stress no end. Buy your tickets and find the bus timetable online. There are also hop-on-hop-off sightseeing tour buses, seen in many cities in the UK and further afield.

TRAINS

The train system is clean and the trains usually run on time. In Cambridge, there are two stations within walking distance of the city. Cambridge Main Station, and Cambridge North. These stations have fast links to London, Gatwick, and Stansted airports and provide services to the East to Birmingham and the seaside in Norfolk. Below is a website address and link to help you plan your travel. If tickets are booked early there are often discounts available.

E-bikes and scooters

E-bikes and scooters can be found on street corners all over the city. Download the Voi app onto your phone to get started.

A BRIEF HISTORY OF THE CITY

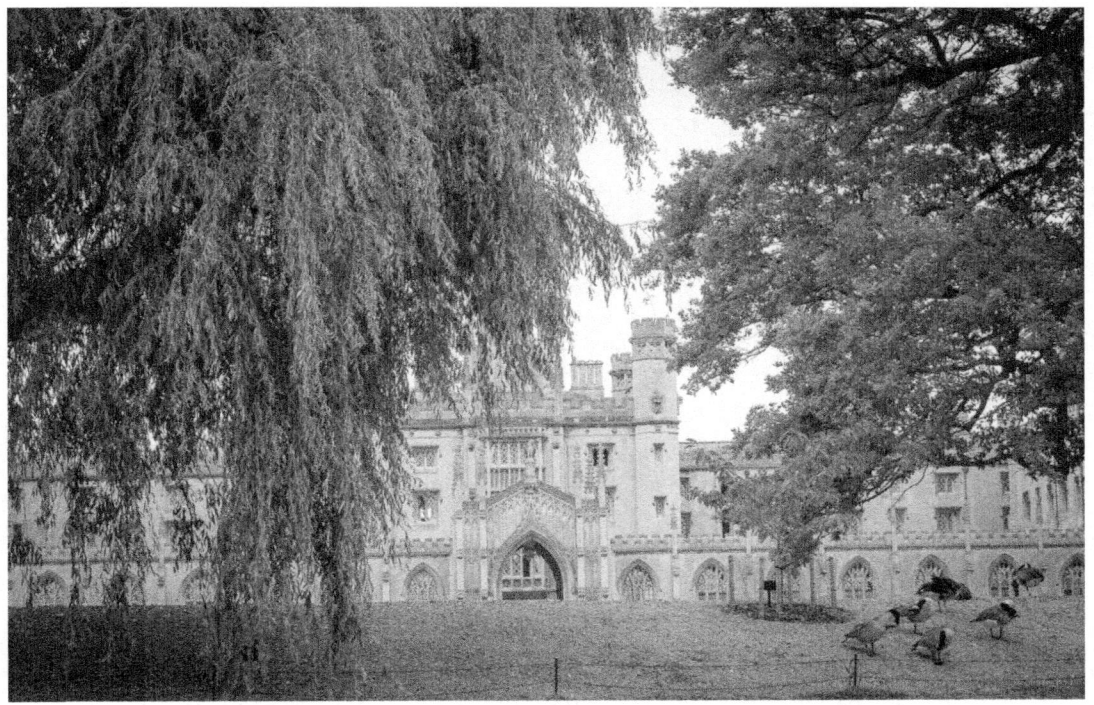

There have been settlements in Cambridge since the Bronze Age, 4000 years ago. The Romans settled here later and built a fort on Castle Hill in the first century. However, as the Roman Empire declined in the fifth century, the castle was abandoned. Cambridge was originally called Granta Brygg and was renamed later as the town grew. An entry in the

Doomsday book in 1086 records a population of 31 households. After this, Cambridge went through many trials of being captured, burned to the ground, and hit by plagues. By the thirteenth century, there were weekly markets and a fair where people from all over would come to buy and sell goods. Midsummer Fair was born at this time and apart from a brief hiatus during the World Wars and the 2020 Covid pandemic, it still runs today. Despite the fact it does not have a cathedral, Cambridge was granted city status in 1951 in recognition of its history and economic and administrative contributions to the lawful government of the United Kingdom.

CAMBRIDGE UNIVERSITY

One of the most prestigious universities in the world, Cambridge University was founded in 1209. It is made up of 31 colleges which are dotted around the city.

Peterhouse, the oldest college, was founded in 1284 and the most recent to be founded were Lucy Cavendish College and Clare Hall which were both founded in 1965.

A shameful fact is that women were not admitted into the colleges until 1869 when the first women's college of Girton was established 2.5 miles out of the city. Cambridge was the last of the well-known education facilities to award women their degrees and did not do so until 1948.

KING'S COLLEGE

King's College and the chapel with its exceptional architecture are found on King's Parade in the heart of the city centre. Inside the immense chapel, you will find world-class fan vaulted ceilings. King's College is recognised for its recording of the Christmas Eve carol service which began in 1918 and has been broadcasted on the radio since 1928.

For some families, listening to Carols from King's is now a tradition that many tune into while stirring the Christmas pudding and preparing for Christmas day. The carols which always begin with Once in Royal David's City are sung by the world-famous King's College Choir.

On Christmas Day, if you queue early enough to get into the candlelit space of the Chapel where the fragrance of Frankincense blends with the angelic voices of the choir. It is alleged that if you close your eyes while listening to the choir on Christmas day, you will be transported to heaven.

TRINITY COLLEGE

Walking north along Kings Parade, the road turns into Trinity Street, where Trinity College Great Gate protects the entrance to the college.

Sir Issac Newton studied here and on the lawn outside Trinity College, you will see an apple tree said to be a graft from the original tree where Newton first saw the apple drop to the ground and his concept of gravity was born.

Folklore tells us that while he was studying at Trinity College his room was one of the ones which overlooked the front lawn where the apple tree now grows.

Trinity Street then changes into St John's Street and as it does so you will find St John's College.

ST JOHN'S COLLEGE

St John's College was founded by Henry VI's mother Lady Margaret Beaufort, in 1511. As with all the colleges in Cambridge, St John's has an impressive list of alumni which add to its glory and prestige, including William Wordsworth and William Wilberforce and to date, a total of ten Nobel prize winners.

THE FITZWILLIAM MUSEUM

Built in 1848 by George Basev in a neoclassical style. The Fitzwilliam was completed by Charles Cockerell after Basev died in 1845. The Fitzwilliam museum is free to enter and is full of inordinate treasures. There are family events and discovery classes and paid-for tours available all week. As you walk up the steps to the entrance to the museum, look up. In England, it is a good practice to look up, as the tops of the buildings can be spectacular.

The Fitzwilliam Museum

THE MARKET

Cambridge has had a market since the Middle Ages and you will find it in the town square every day of the week. On Saturday there are often over 100 stalls where you will find food, plants, bread, clothes, coffee, cakes, and cheeses. It is a noisy and friendly place to buy memorabilia, lunch and snacks and Cambridge branded T-shirts. As you wander in and out of the market stalls the chatter of people speaking assorted and distant languages combined with the smell of exotic spices added to by a hint of rose and Jasmine from the flower stall altogether gives the flavour of an international flair.

The view from Great St Mary's Tower

Pubs

Pubs are a tradition in the UK that is believed to have started in Roman times with the opening of tavernas to serve wine to the legions of Roman soldiers. The name changed to taverns and Inns and public houses opened which began to include food, accommodation, and the locals' favourite drinks on the menu. These names amalgamated together and were shortened to pubs. One of the oldest pubs in England is in Nottingham and is dated 1189 AD. Today in Cambridge you will find countless pubs serving great food.

The Fort St George on the river is a favourite of the locals and visitors to the city. It is also occasionally frequented by the Duke and Duchess of Cambridge.

THE EAGLE

The Eagle is a busy, bustling pub, in the centre of town. Crick and Watson, the famous geneticists, announced the discovery of the DNA Double Helix in 1953.

THE RAF BAR

At the Eagle, you will also find The RAF bar, where pilots from all over the world and some from WWII signed the ceiling to be remembered forever. There is more than enough interesting memorabilia at these places to keep you interested for at least a couple of hours.

THE RAF BAR

FOOD

LUNCH

There are many places to eat lunch and it's possible to walk into most places and ask for a table. However, on a busy summer weekend particularly during university graduations, it is worth booking in advance. Steak & Honour and Doppelganger each serve fast delicious burgers. Bills and The Pint shop are great for good wholesome food.

MICHELIN STARRED FOOD

Midsummer House for a fancy lunch or special event. The two-star Michelin restaurant will delight you with delicious flavours and seasonal ingredients. From town, it is a 10–15-minute walk through the parks to Midsummer Common and along the River Cam, it is situated next to The Fort St George.

MJP@The Shepherds - At the time of writing it does not yet have a Michelin Star however, rumour has it will have one soon, so head along and enjoy the tasty food at pre-star prices! It is located just outside Cambridge in Fen Ditton, a lovely pub worth the 15-minute taxi ride or a cycle ride over the Abbey-Chesterton bridge and through the commons.

CAKES AND CHELSEA BUNS

Fitzbillies Chelsea buns, a Cambridge tradition begun in 1920 by two brothers. Their father Tucker Mason had a shop on Trumpington Street baking bread, so they decided to make cakes and Chelsea buns. Fitzbillies start baking every day at 4 am except for Christmas and New Year's Day. On a busy day, over 800 buns are eaten.

FUDGE

Watch fudge being made and get a free sample at the Fudge Kitchen on King's Parade opposite the entrance to King's College.

AFTERNOON TEA

The most quintessential British pastime if there ever was one. In the 1800s, the 17th Duchess of Bedford, Anna Maria Russell, a lifelong friend of Queen Victoria, began the tradition of having tea and cake at 4 pm each afternoon. As she invited her friends to join her; tea at 4 pm became an established British tradition.

Enjoy delicious small dainty sandwiches and freshly baked cake at Parker's Tavern, The Varsity Hotel, and Brown's Brasserie, all within walking distance of town, and all provide delicious assortments. The Orchard Tea Rooms, in Grantchester, is worth the taxi fare or cycling through Lammas Land.

ONTO THE RIVER

The River Cam is a delightful place for punting, and paddleboarding. There are 26 bridges along its length and walking along the towpaths you will see cows grazing on the commons, swans, and houseboats. The river is an important part of Cambridge life, there have been rowing races and seasonal events on it or close by since the Middle Ages.

It is 155km long and divides loosely into Upper, Middle, and Lower rivers; it spans the counties of Hertfordshire, Essex, and

Cambridgeshire. The river finishes its course by pouring into The River Great Ouse at Ely and flows out towards The Wash and The North Sea at Kings Lynn. The stretch of river that flows through Cambridge has been immortalised in poems, paintings, and stories. Find some of them in Geoffrey Chaucer's Canterbury Tales, The Reeve's Tale, and The Old Vicarage, Grantchester.

THE BACKS, BRIDGES AND COLLEGES

Punting is a must to see the best Cambridge has to offer. For access to the nine bridges along the Backs, you must either enter the colleges (which are not always open to the public and they often charge a fee) or go on a punting tour of "The Backs". However, you can see Magdalene bridge, Silver Street bridge, Garret Hostel, Clare, and the Mathematical bridge from the town.

Punting became popular in the early 20th century. Flat-bottomed boats glide easily on the shallow waters of the River Cam and are propelled along with a long pole dropped onto the riverbed and pushed off. It is a great skill but easily learnt. It is possible to hire your own punt or have a guided tour where you can take a picnic to enjoy while your chauffeur reveals interesting historical stories of the University and life along the Cam. Local students often chauffeur the tours so you will be very well informed. Depending upon the tour you take, it may go under nine of the bridges discussed below and pass by eight of the 31 colleges and three libraries.

MAGDALENE BRIDGE

Magdalene is also known to locals as the Great Bridge. It was the site where the first river crossing, and bridge were built over the river Cam. It is pronounced Mord-lin bridge. Initially made out of wood in Roman times and was once the site of a ducking stool, it linked the North and South London trade routes. The original wooden bridge continually fell into disrepair and finally in the Spring of 1823 an iron bridge double the size of the original wooden bridge was designed. Arthur Browne was the architect, and the engineer was Benjamin Brown; its total cost was about £2,350.

THE BRIDGE OF SIGHS

The Bridge of Sighs is named after the Bridge of Sighs in Venice, Italy. In Venice, the bridge links the palace and the prison. It is part of St John's College and is one of the most photographed bridges in Cambridge. It links St John's College to the West side, known locally as the 'Backs' of Cambridge. It is built in a Victorian Gothic style and was designed by Henry Hutchinson in 1827. Originally it was named 'New Bridge' and was built 9 years after the Mord-Lin iron bridge.

The Bridge has appeared in films and paintings and was made famous by Lord Byron in his book Childe Harold's Pilgrimage. In 1963 it had a car suspended from it by students in an elaborate prank and was featured in the movie The Theory of Everything. However, the bridge is not open to the public and can only be viewed while punting along the River Cam or from the Wren bridge when visiting the college.

MATHEMATICAL BRIDGE

This bridge belongs to Queens College. It was designed by William Etheridge and built by James Essex in 1749. Since then, it has been repaired and rebuilt twice due to weathering of the original oak. The framework used is the tangent and radial trussing.

There are two popular myths about this bridge, one is it is held together without any fixings and students took it apart to discover how it held together and could not put it back without bolts. The other is that it was designed and built by Sir Issac Newton. William Etheridge was a student of Issac Newton, which is where the myth may have originated.

TRINITY BRIDGE

Trinity College is the largest and wealthiest of all the colleges in Cambridge. One of the last acts of Henry VIII was founding Trinity College by combining the existing colleges Michaelhouse and Kings Hall. King Edwards Gate, which houses the Trinity College Clock, has been ticking since 1910.

Many of the bridges in Cambridge were destroyed during the civil war. Trinity is one of those pulled down by Cromwell's men in 1643 and reconstructed from stone; the bridge you see today was constructed by James Essex. Today Trinity bridge is one of the oldest, standing for almost 500 years.

KING'S COLLEGE BRIDGE

King College Bridge is a segmental arch Bridge, designed in 1820 by William Wilkins and built by Francis Braidwood. It is a simple addition to the remarkable King's College. Old English folk law has said the field opposite is the last place where duels were legally allowed to be held in England.

THE WREN BRIDGE AT ST JOHN'S

The Kitchen Bridge or Wren Bridge at St John's is the oldest bridge on the river Cam, named because the kitchens used to be on the opposite side of the river (on The Backs). The bridge is carved from a single block of limestone and was designed by Sir Christopher Wren. While you are punting, it is possible to see the watermarks on the cutwaters of the bridge from historical floods.

CLARE COLLEGE BRIDGE

Clare College bridge is the oldest standing bridge on the Backs and was built by Thomas Grumbold in Ketton stone in 1639. There is a wedge missing from one of the stone finials, history tells us it is because the price for constructing the bridge was not paid in full and the stone mansion took a slice out of the ball to show his distaste at the lack of payment.

GARRETT LANE HOSTEL BRIDGE

Garrett Lane Hostel was built in 1960 and has interesting local names given to it by students. After cyclists' effort to reach the top often result in various noises and exclamations of yes yes yes! It is a public right of way across the river made of a post-tensioned concrete bridge and designed by a student Timothy Morgan who sadly died before the bridge's completion. It is a great place for photos as it has a wonderful view of Clare Bridge.

BRIDGE JUMPING

Bridge jumping or hopping is a sport some students cannot resist, and they make it look easy! However, we do not recommend you try it! Here is how it's done. Climb from a punt onto the bridge above, send your punt under the bridge and then climb back down onto the punt on the other side whilst trying not to fall into the river.

THE CORPUS CLOCK

The Corpus Clock was Invented, designed, and donated to Corpus Christi College by an alumnus, Dr John C Taylor OBE. It was installed in 2008 and is known locally as the time-eater clock.

It is a Chronophage displayed on the corner of Kings Parade and Benet Street in the doorway of the old NatWest Bank, now the exterior of the college library. A stunning feat of engineering, it has no numbers or hands, and the time is told by three rings of LED lights. The outermost ring of lights is the seconds passing, the middle the minutes and the smallest inside ring of lights tells the hour. At the thirty-second mark, the Chronophage will open its mouth and then snap it shut when the minute is over. On the hour chains will shake and a hammer will slam down onto a wooden coffin. Confirming that time is passing, and we will all die! If you can read Latin, you will see the inscription Mundus transit et concupiscentia eius, translated as 'the world and its desires pass away'. The clock is said to have a set of 50 tricks and if you look at it on the 25th of March or November, New Year's Day or Corpus Christi Day you will see some of them, keep your eyes peeled!

CHURCHES

Cambridge has a long Christian heritage where it is believed to have had churches before the 10th century. Now numbering approximately 39 they cater to all denominations. They offer a warm welcome and the magnificent stained-glass windows depict stories of the gospels, great kings, and queens.

THE ROUND CHURCH

The Round Church was built in a Gothic style. Historians believe it was built around 1131. It is located on the roundabout opposite St John's College and is full of interesting history and worth a visit.

THE CHURCH OF ST BENET

The Church of St Benet is where people have worshipped for over a thousand years and was believed to have been built in 1020. Until the 1600's students were called to lectures by the bells. Each Friday there are practice bell ringing sessions, not open to the public but lovely to listen to. This church is full of historical artefacts.

The university colleges have produced 18 Archbishops of Canterbury and Cambridge has the highest number of resident clergy per capita in the UK.

GREAT ST MARY'S

To study at Cambridge, it is said that all the undergraduates of the University must live within three miles of The Church of St Mary the Great.

This church is 800 years old and has been designed in a perpendicular style. It is open every day, but Sundays are reserved for church services.

For a fee, it is possible to climb the 123 steps of the bell tower and once you reach the top you will gain a spectacular view of the city.

The Bell Tower Of Great St Mary's

A View Of King's College From Great St Mary's

ROWING

There has been rowing on the river Cam since the 1800s. Today in Cambridge there are town rowing clubs, and each university college has its own women's and men's teams.

Each morning from as early as 6 am it is possible to find both the women's and men's teams rowing on the river between The Victoria Bridge and Baits Bite Lock. Most months of the year there are events on the river, find them on the Cambridge Rowing Association website.

If you would like to row, contact one of the town clubs to enquire if you can book a class.

HOUSEBOATS AND BOATHOUSES

On the river In between Fort St George pub and the Cutter Ferry Bridge on Midsummer Common, you will find most of the University boathouses and the town rowing clubs. A 10-minute walk from the city centre will take you to the banks of the River Cam where during the weekends or early mornings you can sit on a bench and watch the rowers training and getting ready to row on the river.

SWANS

Today all swans in the UK belong to the Queen of England. In 1246 Henry III decreed they all belonged to the crown and so it was. Swans are known throughout the world for their strength, fidelity, and grace, and they can fly at speed.

According to folklore, swans sing most beautifully before they die and the phrase for a swan song is often used at the final performance of an actor, singer, composer, or poet who leaves in style. References to its use are found in the works of Plato, Aristotle, and Cicero, and Shakespeare used it in several plays. The cygnets and ducklings usually hatch in May and watching and feeding them along the river is a great pastime.

THE TOUR

Choose where you start and end the tour and begin your day with a relaxing punt or reverse the four steps and end with the punt, either way, the tour is fantastic. Scudamore's punting has been working on the River Cam for over 100 years. You will be given a great overview of the city and an unforgettable tour of the local history. Take a picnic and or drinks with you and stylishly enjoy your tour. Check the websites of all the recommended places for opening times and costs of extra tours, so you are well planned and can relax and enjoy your day.

WALKING DIRECTIONS FOR THE TOUR

1. Start on Bridge Street, at the punting station next to Magdalene Bridge.

2. Go on a punting tour of the Backs of Cambridge.

3. If you return from the punt and feel peckish, cross over Bridge St and go into Fitzbillies for coffee and a traditional sticky Chelsea bun.

4. Keep on your left and walk away from Magdalene Bridge and the river along Bridge Street towards the town centre.

5. After approximately 3 minutes and 220 yards, you will see The Round Church on your left. This is where you begin the walking tour, take as much or as little time as you need for your journey and stop to take photographs. Visit the places pointed out in this tour, you will then have a wonderful overview and understanding of Cambridge.

6. With your back to the Round Church, cross the road and walk along St John's Street.

7. Keep to the right of the footpath and take a tour with a guide from St John's College.

8. Come out of St John's walk further to Trinity College and take a tour of the College if available.

9. St John's Street will change into Kings Parade where you will find King's College.

10. On the left-hand side of the road, you will see the Corpus Clock on the corner of Benet Street.

11. Kings Parade changes into Trumpington Street where you will see 'the other Fitzbillies' coffee shop. Stop in for some refreshments as the next stop is The Fitzwilliam Museum.

12. The Fitzwilliam is found on your right when you continue along Trumpington Street for a further four minutes.

13. It is possible to veer off the beaten track and find more of the treasures of Cambridge but if you only have one day, this is the tour for you.

FAMILY ACTIVITIES AND LINKS

There is a marvellous array of interesting and educational activities specifically targeted at children. These activities are put on by the local museums, which have too many treasures to write about. If you have time to plan, search for the individual websites online and find the times and activities that suit you and your family as many events need to be booked due to the high demand. The Tourist Information Centre has a wealth of knowledge, tours, guides, and information. Drop by to plan theatre trips and book tickets to events you want to experience.

Have great fun and learn lots on a great history tour with a difference!
https://terribletours.co.uk History Link

https://opendomesday.org/place/TL4458/cambridge

Here is the vital link you need to plan an awesome day out in Cambridge for the family https://www.museums.cam.ac.uk/whats-on

The Fitzwilliam Museum
https://fitzmuseum.cam.ac.uk/learning/families

The Museum of Zoology
https://www.museum.zoo.cam.ac.uk/visit-us/visiting-families

The Polar Museum, Scott Polar Institute
https://www.spri.cam.ac.uk/museum/access/

The Botanic Gardens https://www.botanic.cam.ac.uk/whats-on/

Duxford Air Museum In the village of Duxford 10 miles or a short train journey to Whittlesford out of town but well worth a visit particularly if there is a special event on you like WW11 and or aircraft.
https://www.iwm.org.uk/visits/iwm-duxford/whats-o

THEATRE

Cambridge Arts Theatre and independent theatre in the heart of the city. Find the box office on St Edwards Passage.

https://www.cambridgeartstheatre.com

ACD Theatre

Beginning life in 1855 this is the oldest playhouse in Britain. It has a wonderful history with performances originating in the back room of the Hoop Inn. This is a theatre to go to with impressive alumni such as Emma Thompson, Peter Cook, Stephen Fry, Hugh Laurie, and Rachel Weisz.

FESTIVALS

There are various festivals on the summer calendar in Cambridge. Take a picnic and a blanket to sit on to see a magical performance of Shakespeare in the University College gardens, which are often closed and out of view from the public.

MUSIC

By the river or a recital in the chapels, you will be delighted with the plethora of offerings for a relaxed summer evening out in the city

Night Clubs

Night Clubs for when you want to go out and let your hair down. There are some great places ranging in cost and style.

HIDDEN GEMS AND SECRETS

Cows on the Common! There has been grazing for cows and horses on Midsummer Common since the 12th century. A parliamentary act in 1965 gives people who live or own land in Cambridge permission to graze their animals.

Not being allowed to keep dogs in the student accommodation it is rumoured that Lord Byron kept a bear instead. Oliver Cromwell was buried in Westminster Abbey in London. However, his skull was dug up and is now buried in Cambridge, can you find out where?
Jesus Green Lido is the longest outdoor swimming pool in Europe.
Other Bridges And Locks

1. A14 Road Bridge
2. Abbey Chesterton Bridge
3. Baits Bite Lock
4. Coe Fen
5. Crusoe
6. Cutter Ferry Bridge
7. Elizabeth Way Bridge
8. Fen Causeway
9. Fort St George Bridge
10. Green Dragon Bridge

11. Jesus Lock footbridge
12. Middle River at Mill Pond
13. Riverside Bridge is hoped to be renamed the Equiano Bridge after a famous man who lived nearby.
14. Silver Street
15. The Railway Bridge
16. Trumpington Bridge
17. Victoria Avenue Bridge

Acknowledgements

Hannah Glover and Joseph Lewis for punting us along the backs while Vanessa Champion captured the stunning architecture and life you see in the photographs. Megan Glover for her unwavering encouragement and proofreading. Without these wonderful people, there would be no mini guide to Cambridge, a useful and easy way to see and experience the wonders of this beautiful city.

Printed in Great Britain
by Amazon